A Short Story

About the Boy Lae\`ula
and the Rare Birds
at Alaka\`i, Kōke\`e, Kaua\`i

By Keahi Manea
Illustrated by Kayleigh Chalkowski

Copyright © 2018 by Kaua`i Forest Bird Recovery Project. All rights reserved. No part of this publication may be reproduced, distributed, or transmitted in any form or by any means, including photocopying, recording, or other electronic or mechanical methods, without the prior written permission of the publisher, except in the case of brief quotations embodied in critical reviews and certain other noncommercial uses permitted by copyright law. For permission requests, write to KFBRP at the address below.

Illustrations © 2018 by Kayleigh Chalkowski

Kaua`i Forest Bird Recovery Project
P.O. Box 27
3751 Hanapepe Rd
Hanapepe, HI 96716
(808) 335-5078
www.kauaiforestbirds.org

ISBN: 9781986677677

Author's Preface

In early 2011, Dr. Lisa Crampton contacted me with a request that our hula institute kōkua the Kauaʻi Forest Bird Recovery Project by providing a Hawaiian blessing for their spring research season.

Thus began an enduring collaboration between KFBRP and Ka ʻImi Naʻauaao o Hawaiʻi Nei Institute, of which I am Secretary. The Institute's hula teachers and students have learned about Kauaʻi endangered native birds and Project staff and volunteers have deepened their understanding of Hawaiian protocols and values.

As a life-long student of Hawaiian language, I have worked to promote its use in everyday life. Writing this story was a way to promote use of Hawaiian while also increasing awareness among children and adults of the issues facing Kaua`i's endangered birds. The publication of this book is a gift to KFBRP to help with fund-raising. I gratefully and humbly acknowledge the kōkua of my hula and Hawaiian language teachers, Roselle Keli`ihonipua Bailey, Paul Koki Williams and Byron Hōkūlani Cleeland. Writing this story begun as a class project in Kumu Koki Williams' Hawaiian language class at Kaua`i Community College in 2014. His teaching has deepened my understanding of Hawaiian language as he has guided me through the creation of this manuscript. Mahalo nui loa e Kumu Koki!

Sally Jo Keahi Manea

He haumana `eleu a nīele `o Lae`ula ma ke Kula
Ha`aha`a `o Kekaha. Ua lohe maila `o ia he mau
manu laha`ole `ōiwi ma ka nahele `o Kōke`e. Nui
kona makemake i ka `ike maka i kēia mau manu
kaka`ikahi.

Lae`ula is a clever and curious student at Kekaha
Elementary School. He heard that there are
some rare native birds in the forest in Kōke`e.
He really wanted to see these rare birds.

Birds
of
Hawaii

No laila, pi`i kuahiwi `o ia i Kōke`e a hiki i
Alaka`i, kahi ona i hui pū ai me kekahi pua`a e
`eku ana ma lalo o ke kumu la`au `ōhi`a. Hea
aku `o Lae`ula, "Aloha e Pua`a, `o wau `o Lae`ula,
ke `imi nei i ka manu laha`ole i kapa `ia he
`akeke`e. He hulu melemele a `ōma`o kona. Ua
`ike paha `oe iā ia?"
Pane mai ka pua`a, "Kā! Mai ho`oluhi `oe ia`u.
`Ono wau i nā mea kanu `ōiwi o lalo nei."

So he went hiking up in Kōke`e in the Alaka`i
swamp where he met a wild pig rooting under
an `ōhi`a tree. Lae`ula called out, "Hello there,
Pua`a, I'm Lae`ula. I'm looking for a rare bird
called the `akeke`e. It has yellow-green feathers.
Have you perhaps seen one?"
The pig answered, "Ha! Don`t bother me. I'm
hungry for these native plants under here."

6

Pi`i hou a`ela `o Lae`ula a hiki i ke kahawai `o Kawaikōī. Ua
lohe `o ia, he wahi kūpono nā pali e hana pūnana ai nā manu
puaiohi. Ua `ike `o ia i kekahi `iole e iho mai ana mai ka pali
mai me kekahi mea i pa`a ma kona miki`ao.

"Aloha kakahiaka e `Iole, he aha kēnā?"  Pane mai `o `Iole, "I
`aina kakahiaka kēia hua manu na`u. `Ū, moni ku`u hā`ae!"
Ha`i aku `o Lae`ula, "Mai hea mai kēnā hua manu?"  Iā `Iole e
nānā a`e ana i ka pūnana manu, ua `ike `o Lae`ula he manu
puaiohi ma luna e nuku ana iā lāua. Kaumaha `o Lae`ula akā
na`e mau kona holo ma ke ala hele.

Lae`ula continued hiking until he reached Kawaikōī Stream.
He had heard that the steep cliffs of this place were where the
puaiohi birds nested. He saw a rat descending the cliff with
something in his paws.

"Good morning to you `Iole, what have you got there?" `Iole
replied, "This egg is for my breakfast. Hmmm, my mouth is
watering!" Lae`ula said, "Where is that egg from?" While
`Iole looked up at the bird nest, Lae`ula looked up and saw a
puaiohi bird scolding them. Lae`ula was sad, but continued
along the trail.

Iā ia e holo ana ma luna o ke ala papa o Alaka`i, lele maila ka makika a ku`u ma kona lima. Ha`i aku `o Lae`ula, "Aloha e Makika.  Pū`iwa au e `ike iā `oe ma luna nei ma Alaka`i." Pane mai `o Makika, "`Ae, he malihini au.  I ka wā ma mua, `a`ole hiki ia`u ke lele i kahi ki`eki`e e like me kēia, akā ma muli o ka mehana o kēia wahi i hiki ai ia`u ke lele ma `ane` i kēia manawa. Makemake au i ke koko `ono o ka manu `akikiki!" Kaumaha `o Lae`ula akā na`e mau kona holo ma ke ala papa.

As he walked along the Alaka`i boardwalk trail, a mosquito landed on his arm. Lae`ula said, "Greetings Makika, I'm surprised to see you up here in Alaka`i." Makika answered, "Yes, I'm a newcomer here. In the past, I haven't been able to fly to this elevation, but because this place is warmer now, I can fly here. I like the tasty blood of the `akikiki bird!" Lae`ula was sad, but continued along the boardwalk.

11

Iā Lae`ula e holo mua ana i ka panepo`o `o Kilohana, no`ono`o ihola `o ia i nā manu laha`ole o Alaka`i. "Auē! Ma ka honua holo`oko`a, noho `oukou ma `ane`i wale nō. He mau manu pono`ī o ka `āina `oukou a kokoke e halapohe, ea. `Auē!"

As Lae`ula continued on to the summit and the Kilohana Lookout, he thought about the rare native birds of Alaka`i. "Oh my! In the whole world, you birds live only here. You are truly native birds of the land, yet you are close to extinction. Oh dear!"

`Emo`ole, lohe `o ia i nā leo mākua i mua ona.  I kona huli `ana i ke ala kīke`e, aia kekahi kāne a me kekahi wahine e kū ana ma laila. Ua ha`i mai ka wahine, "Aloha e ke keiki. He lā nani nō kēia no ka pi`i kuahiwi, a no ke aha pupuku nei kou lae?" Pane `o Lae`ula, "`Ae, nani nō, ua pi`i kuahiwi au e `ike i ku`u mau manu minamina, `o ka `akeke`e, `o ka `akikiki a me ka puaiohi. Akā na`e, `o ka hapanui o nā mea a`u i `ike ai, `o ia nā mea e pilikia nei lākou, `o ka pua`a, `o ka `iole a me ka makika."

Not long after, he heard adult voices in front of him. When he came around a turn in the trail, a man and a woman were standing there.
The woman said, "Hello there, boy. It's a beautiful day for hiking, so why are you frowning?"
Lae`ula answered, "Yes, it is a nice day. I came hiking to see my favorite treasured birds, the `akeke`e, `akikiki, and puaiohi. But I have mostly seen the things that cause trouble for them, the pig, the rat, and the mosquito."

Ha`i ka wahine, "`Ae, he pilikia ko kēia mau manu. Akā, ke kōkua nei mākou, ka po`e o ke Kaua`i Forest Bird Recovery Project a me ko mākou mau hoa kōkua, i kēia mau manu `ōiwi laha`ole i `ole lākou e nalowale. Mai kaumaha `oe e Lae`ula, ua koe nō kēia mau manu, a hiki iā kākou ke kōkua iā lākou.  Ke kūkulu nei mākou i nā pā i mea e pa`a ai nā pua`a ma waho aku o kekahi mau wahi ma Alaka`i a e hana ana mākou i mau pūnana i hiki `ole i ka `iole ke komo. E hiki koke mai ana ka wā a kākou e ho`ēmi ai i ka nui o nā makika."

The woman said, "Yes, these birds are in trouble. But the Kaua`i Forest Bird Recovery Project staff and their partners are helping the rare native birds so they don't become extinct. Don't be sad, Lae`ula, the birds are still here and we can help them. We are building fences to keep the pigs out of some places in Alaka`i, and we're building nests that rats can't enter. Soon, the time will come when we are able to reduce the mosquito population."

`Emo`ole, ua maka`ala ke kanaka, a kīki`i kona
po`o, me ka ho`olohe `ana aku. "Nānā i luna e
Lae`ula, aia he `akeke`e ma`ō! E kali iki a e lohe
paha `ia ka `akikiki kekahi. E aho nui kākou."

Hau`oli `o Lae`ula e `ike maka i nā manu `ōiwi
o Alaka`i.  `Oli`oli `o ia i ka `ike mōakaaka `ana
i nā `āina ma lalo o Kilohana, `o Wainiha, `o
Lumaha`i, a `o Hanalei a hiki loa i Kīlauea. He lā
nani nō kēia!

Pīpī holo ka`ao.

Not long afterward, the man became attentive, tilted his head and listened. "Look up there Lae`ula, there is an `akeke`e! If we wait a bit, we might hear an `akikiki too. Let's be patient."

Lae`ula was very happy to see with his own eyes these native birds of Alaka`i. He was filled with joy as he turned to see clearly the lands below Kilohana Lookout, all the way to Hanalei. This was a beautiful day!

Kaua`i Forest Bird Recovery Project

The Kaua`i Forest Bird Recovery Project is a Hawai`i Department of Land and Natural Resources, Division of Forestry and Wildlife (DOFAW) program in collaboration with the Pacific Studies Cooperative Unit of the University of Hawai`i and Garden Island Resource Conservation and Development, Inc. KFBRP receives funding from DOFAW, the U.S. Fish and Wildlife Service, and private and not-for-profit donors.

We are committed to promoting knowledge, appreciation, and conservation of Kaua`i's native forest birds, all of which are unique to Hawai`i; several are found only on Kaua`i. We seek to understand the ecology of the birds of Kaua`i, the impacts of the many threats they face, and the potential of different management strategies for recovering their populations. We strive to communicate these issues to the general public through materials like this book, our website (kauaiforestbirds. org) and Facebook page, and through outreach events and classroom presentations on Kaua`i.

When the project began in 2003, we focused on the endangered puaiohi, or Small Kaua`i Thrush, the only species listed as endangered at the time. In 2010, our efforts expanded to include two more of Kaua`i's endemic songbirds, the `akikiki and the `akeke`e, after they were listed as endangered by the U.S. Fish and Wildlife Service. All of our research and conservation is conducted on Kaua`i's Alaka`i Plateau, the only place where these birds are still to be found.

Learn More About Kaua`i's Native Forest Birds!

The **`Akeke`e** is found only on Kaua`i. The tips of its bill are slightly offset, allowing it to wedge open leaf buds for small insects. Once common, the population has plummeted and is now estimated at fewer than 1000 birds.
Status: Critically Endangered

The **`Akikiki**, or **Kaua`i Creeper** numbers fewer than 500 birds. While it may appear plain, this bird is highly charismatic, doing acrobatics around tree branches in search of food.
Status: Critically Endangered

The **Puaiohi** or **Small Kaua`i Thrush** is a secretive bird and only found on Kaua`i. With fewer than 500 individuals, observers have to hike deep into the Alaka`i to patiently wait for a lucky sighting along streams with steep cliffs.
Status: Critically Endangered

The **`I`iwi** is among the most iconic of the Hawaiian birds, thanks to its bright red and black colors and long orange bill. It can be found on all main Hawaiian Islands, but recent studies on Kaua`i are showing an alarming decline in numbers.
Status: Vulnerable

While the **Kaua`i `Elepaio** has close relatives on other Hawaiian islands, this species is unique to Kaua`i. These birds are experts at zipping through the air and catching flying insects while in mid-flight. The Kaua`i `Elepaio's population is relatively stable.

Status: Vulnerable

The **`Anianiau** is the smallest of the honeycreeper species; its weight is equivalent to four pennies! While they are increasingly rare in Kaua`i's forests, their bright yellow plumage is unmistakable.

Status: Vulnerable

The **Kaua`i `Amakihi** has relatives on O`ahu, Maui, and the Big Island, but this species only lives on Kaua`i. It is a generalist species, and uses its large, down-curved bill to probe for insects, drink nectar, and pick berries. Due to recent population crashes, there is growing concern for this unique bird.

Status: Vulnerable

Still common on all Hawaiian Islands, the **`Apapane** is a real treat to see. Its black and red feathers blend in perfectly with `ōhi`a trees, sometimes making it hard to spot them in the treetops. Lucky for the observer, they are very vocal!

Status: Least Concern

About the Author

Sally Jo Keahi Manea is a retired epidemiologist, nurse, and life-long student of Hawaiian culture, language and hula. Since the 1970's, she has been active with groups involved in the restoration of Kaua`i native habitat and cultural sites.  She lives in Wailua Homesteads on Kaua`i with her husband Tepairu Manea.

About the Illustrator

Kayleigh is a scientist and illustrator. In 2013, she earned a B.Sc. in Biology from Cornell University and since then has worked with birds in Hawaii, Texas, New York and Borneo. In her artwork, she celebrates the beauty of nature while presenting imagery from her observations as a field biologist. In spring 2017 she curated the group exhibition "The Endangered Ark" in Honolulu, Hawai`i to bring together activism and the arts to speak out for endangered species. View her portfolio at kayleighchalkowski.com.

Kaua`i Forest Bird Recovery Project

P.O. Box 27
3751 Hanapepe Rd
Hanapepe, HI 96716
(808) 335-5078
www.kauaiforestbirds.org

www.ingramcontent.com/pod-product-compliance
Lightning Source LLC
Chambersburg PA
CBHW040201240726
48664CB00002B/789